Copyright © 2023 Hayde Miller
All rights reserved. This book or any portion thereof may not be reproduced or used in any manner whatsoever without the express written permission of the publisher except for the use of brief quotations in a book review.

ISBN 979-8-9878563-4-5

WITH GOD ALL
THINGS ARE POSSIBLE.

- MATTHEW 19:26

I AM HER

♥

DAILY REFLECTIONS

DATE

> **BE STILL, AND KNOW THAT *I AM* GOD.**
>
> —PSALM 46:10

DAILY REFLECTIONS

DATE

BUT THE LORD
STOOD WITH ME AND
GAVE ME STRENGTH.

• 2 TIMOTHY 4:17

ADJUST YOUR CROWN AND HANDLE IT.

DAILY REFLECTIONS

DATE

I WILL WALK BY
FAITH EVEN WHEN I
CANNOT SEE.

- 2 CORINTHAINS 5:7

THE DREAM IS FREE
THE HUSTLE IS SOLD
SEPARATELY.

♥

DAILY REFLECTIONS

DATE

> FAITH CAN MOVE MOUNTAINS.

-MATTHEW 17:20

MELANIN
♥

DAILY REFLECTIONS

DATE

YOU ARE
GOD'S
MASTERPIECE

-ESPHESIANS 2:10

ALWAYS BRING VALUE.

♥

DAILY REFLECTIONS

DATE

GOD IS OUR REFUGE AND STRENGTH, A VERY PRESENT HELP IN TROUBLE.

-PSALM 46:1

NO ONE CAN LOVE YOU MORE THAN YOURSELF.

♥

DAILY REFLECTIONS

DATE

I CAN DO EVERTHING
THROUGH CHRIST
WHO GIVES ME
STRENGTH.

-PHILLIPPIANS 4:13

DAILY REFLECTIONS

DATE

GOD RENEW MY ENERGY

I FEEL TIRED AND WEAK.

-PSALM 103:5

DAILY REFLECTIONS

DATE

IT IS WHO ARMS ME
WITH STRENGTH AND
KEEPS MY WAY
SECURE.

-PSALM 18:32

ANY COLOR FITS YOU ROCK WITH PRIDE.

♥

DAILY REFLECTIONS

DATE

PRAY MORE
WORRY LESS.

-MATTHEW 6:34

BLACK MAGIC
♥

DAILY REFLECTIONS

DATE

ASK FOR ME AND
MY HOUSE WE WILL SERVE
THE
LORD.

-JOSHUA 24:15

DAILY REFLECTIONS

DATE

HE IS WITH YOU.

HEBREWS 13:5

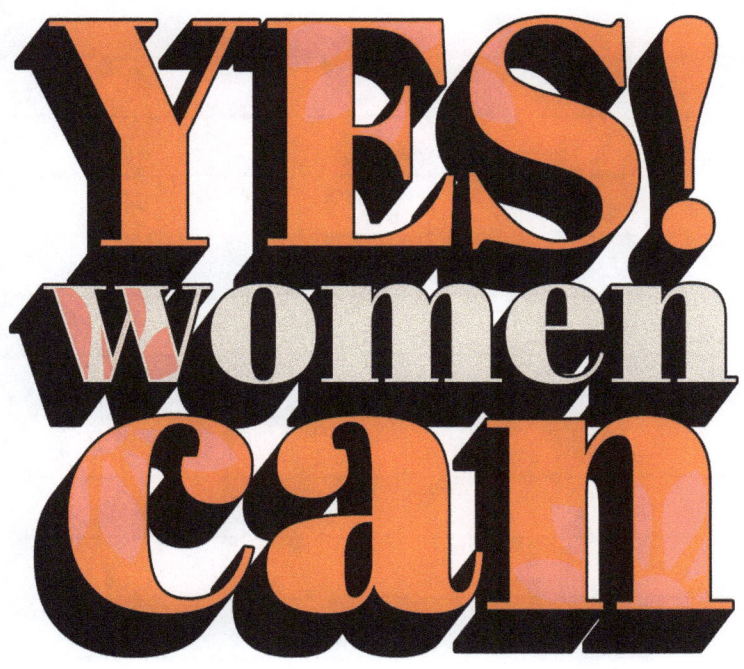

DAILY REFLECTIONS

DATE

>

GOD HAS NOT
GIVEN US A SPIRIT OF
FEAR.

-2 TIMOTHY 1:7

THE STRONGEST ACTIONS FOR A WOMAN IS TO LOVE HERSELF. BE HERSELF AND SHINE AMONGST THOSE WHO NEVER BELIEVED SHE COULD.
-MISSFIYAH FIAH

DAILY REFLECTIONS

DATE

WE CAN MAKE OUR PLANS,

BUT THE LORD DETERMINES OUR STEPS.

PROVERBS 16:9

NEVER APOLOGIZE FOR BEING YOU

DAILY REFLECTIONS

DATE

WE LOVE BECAUSE HE FIRST LOVED US.

-1 JOHN 4:19 (NIV)

YOUR BODY IS A TEMPLE,
EMBRACE IT.

DAILY REFLECTIONS

DATE

> **YOUR WORD IS A LAMP** TO GUIDE MY FEET AND A LIGHT FOR MY PATH.

-PSALM 119-105

·NO TIME FOR·
DRAMA

DAILY REFLECTIONS

DATE

> ## MIGHTIER THAN THE WAVES
> OF THE SEA IS HIS LOVE FOR YOU.
>
> —PSALM 93:4

DAILY
REFLECTIONS

DATE

HATERED STIRS UP STRIFE,
BUT LOVE COVERS ALL SINS.

-PROVERBS 10:12

TURNING YOUR BACK WILL
NEVER SOLVE THE PROBLEM

♥

DAILY REFLECTIONS

DATE

GOD IS WITHIN
HER SHE WILL
NOT FALL.

—PSALM 46:5

POSE WITH GRATITUDE AND GRACE ♥

DAILY REFLECTIONS

DATE

SHE IS
FEARLESS.

-PROVERBS 31:25

GIVING YOURSELF FLOWERS CAN VALIDATE YOUR INNER- SELF CONFIDENCE

> ## DO THE RIGHT THINGS
> ### FOR THE RIGHT REASONS.
>
> —MATTHEW 6:1-4, 5-8

DAILY REFLECTION IS PROGRESS.

DAILY REFLECTIONS

DATE

> PRIORITZE ETERNAL THINGS,
>
> NOT TEMPORAL
>
> ONES.

-MATTHEW 6:19-24

SELF-CARE IS YOUR FUEL TO DAILY SUCCESS.

DAILY REFLECTIONS

DATE

> YOU ARE WHAT YOU BELIVE YOU ARE. *you*

— JOSEPH BENNER

SIT DOWN AND OBSERVE. EVERYTHING AROUND YOU TELLS A STORY.
♥

DAILY REFLECTIONS

DATE

> **STAY TRUE TO
> YOUR
> CONVICTIONS.**
>
> -MATTHEW 7:13-20

REMEMBER YOU ARE THE BASE INGREDIENTS IS NEEDED TO MAKE ALL COLORS.

♥

DAILY
REFLECTIONS

DATE

FORGIVE
OTHERS.

-MATTHEW 6:14-15

LOOK AS I RISE TO THE TOP OF PEACE, HAPPINESS & SELF-LOVE

♥

DAILY REFLECTIONS

DATE

> HIS GRACE
> IS
> ENOUGH.

-CORINTHIANT 12:9

SHINE EVEN WHEN THE SUN IS NOT OUT.

♥

DAILY REFLECTIONS

DATE

> ❝
>
> YOU ARE WHAT
> YOU BELIVE YOU
> ARE.
> *you*
>
> — JOSEPH BENNER

DAILY REFLECTIONS

DATE

> **LOVE NEVER GIVES UP.**
>
> • 1 COR 13:4-7

QUEEN AND NOTHING LESS.

DAILY
REFLECTIONS

DATE

BE JOYFUL
ALWAYS.

-THESSALONIANS 5:16

KNOWLEADGE IS WEALTH.

♥

DAILY
REFLECTIONS

DATE

I AM WITH YOU
AND WILL WATCH OVER YOU WHEREVER YOU
GO.

-GENESIS 28:15

www.ingramcontent.com/pod-product-compliance
Lightning Source LLC
Chambersburg PA
CBHW050456110426
42743CB00017B/3380